W9-AYN-042

daybook, *n.* a book in which the events of the day are recorded; *specif.* a journal or diary

DAYBOOK
of Critical Reading and Writing

AUTHOR

VICKI SPANDEL

CONSULTING AUTHORS

RUTH NATHAN

LAURA ROBB

Great Source Education Group
a Houghton Mifflin Company
Wilmington, Massachusetts

AUTHOR

Vicki Spandel, director of Write Traits, provides training to writing teachers both nationally and internationally. A former teacher and journalist, Vicki is author of more than twenty books, including the new third edition of *Creating Writers* and the *Write Traits Classroom Kits®*.

CONSULTING AUTHORS

Ruth Nathan, one of the authors of *Writers Express* and *Write Away*, is the author of many professional books and articles on literacy. She currently teaches in third grade as well as consults with numerous schools and organizations on reading.

Laura Robb, author of *Teaching Reading in Middle School, Teaching Reading in Social Studies, Science, and Math*, and *Literacy Links: The Emergent Literacy At-Risk Children Need* has taught language arts at Powhatan School in Boyce, Virginia, for more than thirty-five years. She also mentors and coaches teachers in Virginia public schools and speaks at conferences throughout the country.

Copyright © 2003 by Great Source Education Group, Inc. All rights reserved.

No part of this work may be reproduced or transmitted in any form or by any means, electronic or mechanical, including photocopying and recording, or by any information storage or retrieval system without the prior written permission of the copyright owner unless such copying is expressly permitted by federal copyright law. With the exception of non-profit transcription in Braille, Great Source Education Group is not authorized to grant permission for further uses of copyrighted selections reprinted in this text without the permission of their owners. Permission must be obtained from the individual copyright owners as identified herein. Address requests for permission to make copies of Great Source material only to Great Source Education Group, Inc., 181 Ballardvale Street, Wilmington, MA 01887.

Great Source® is a registered trademark of Houghton Mifflin Company.

Printed in the United States of America

International Standard Book Number: 0-669-50098-4

1 2 3 4 5 6 7 8 9 10 – BA – 06 05 04 03 02

Focus/Strategy Lesson

Author
Literature

TABLE OF CONTENTS

Introduction: Active Reading PAGES 7–12

Mark the Reading
Predict What Happens
Ask Questions
Draw What You See
Review

Edward Marshall **8**
from *Tuesday's Lunch* (FICTION)

UNIT 1

Reading Stories PAGES 13–28

characters 1. Character Clues

Jean Van Leeuwen **14**
"Growing Up" from
More Tales of Amanda Pig

setting 2. Where Are We?

Cynthia Rylant **20**
from *Henry and Mudge Under the Yellow Moon* (FICTION)

plot 3. What Is Happening?

Angela Shelf Medearis **24**
"The Scary Movie" from *The Adventures of Sugar and Junior* (FICTION)

© GREAT SOURCE. COPYING IS PROHIBITED.

Focus/Strategy   Lesson   **Author**
                                                  Literature

TABLE OF CONTENTS

UNIT 2

Reading Nonfiction   PAGES **29–40**

main idea	1. Looking for the Main Idea	**Allan Fowler** from *The Sun Is Always Shining Somewhere* (NONFICTION)	**30**
main idea/ details	2. Big Ideas and Small	**Melvin Berger** from *Germs Make Me Sick!* (NONFICTION)	**34**
retelling	3. What's It About?	**Paul Showers** from *Sleep Is for Everyone* (NONFICTION)	**38**

UNIT 3

Reading Authors   PAGES **41–58**

characters	1. Learning About Characters	**Wade Hudson** from *Jamal's Busy Day* (FICTION)	**42**
word choice	2. Authors Choose Words	**Jama Kim Rattigan** from *Truman's Aunt Farm* (FICTION)	**47**
plot	3. What a Problem!	**Arnold Lobel** from "The Wishing Well" (FICTION)	**53**

© GREAT SOURCE. COPYING IS PROHIBITED.

Focus/Strategy	Lesson	Author Literature

TABLE OF CONTENTS

UNIT 4

Reading Poetry — PAGES 59–70

rhyme	1. Time . . . Dime . . . Rhyme!	**Mary Ann Hoberman** "Changing" (POETRY)	**60**
word fun	2. This Poem Makes Me Feel . . .	**Walter Dean Myers** "Jeannie Had a Giggle" (POETRY)	**63**
word choice	3. Word Pictures	**Nikki Grimes** "Big Plans" (POETRY)	**66**

UNIT 5

Reading Nonfiction — PAGES 71–86

retelling	1. What Does It Mean?	**Paula Z. Hogan** from *The Elephant* (NONFICTION)	**72**
sequencing	2. Know What Happens	**Sabrina Crewe** from *The Alligator* (NONFICTION)	**77**
using graphic organizers	3. Read to Understand	**Kimberly Brubaker Bradley** from *Pop! A Book About Bubbles* (NONFICTION)	**82**

© GREAT SOURCE. COPYING IS PROHIBITED.

Focus/Strategy   Lesson   **Author**
                                           Literature

TABLE OF CONTENTS

UNIT 6

	Reading Authors	PAGES **87–106**
problem-solution	1. What's the Problem?	**Gary Soto** 88 from *Too Many Tamales* (FICTION)
connect— form opinions	2. What Do I Think?	**Simon James** 96 from *Dear Mr. Blueberry* (FICTION)
theme	3. What's It All Mean?	**Jane Yolen** 100 from *Owl Moon* (FICTION)
	Glossary	107
	Acknowledgments	108
	Index	110

6

© GREAT SOURCE. COPYING IS PROHIBITED.

Introduction: Active Reading

Active readers think a lot when they read. They ask questions. They mark the page. They imagine pictures as they read. They guess what will happen next. When you read, be an active reader too.

© GREAT SOURCE. COPYING IS PROHIBITED.

Mark the Reading

When you read, mark the important parts. You can underline, circle, or highlight the parts you think are important.

Find the important parts and mark them.

from *Tuesday's Lunch*
by Edward Marshall

Tuesday was sunny and hot.

"You may eat lunch outside," said Miss Moon.

"Let's go!" cried the class.

And they all went outside.

Fox, Carmen, and Dexter sat down and opened their lunches.

"Ugh!" said Carmen. "Tuna fish!"

"Ugh!" said Fox. "Tuna fish!"

"Oh, no!" said Dexter. "Tuna fish!"

© GREAT SOURCE. COPYING IS PROHIBITED.

2 Predict What Happens

As you read, think about what will happen next. This is called **predicting**. Then, read to find out if you were right.

Try to predict what will happen as you read.

from ***Tuesday's Lunch***
by Edward Marshall

"Let's throw our lunches away," said Fox.

"Let's do!" said the others.

They were so proud of themselves.

"This will teach Mom," said Dexter.

But soon they were very hungry.

"Whose idea was this anyway?" said Fox.

"Guess!" said his friends.

After school they ran to look for their sandwiches.

They will get in trouble.

© GREAT SOURCE. COPYING IS PROHIBITED.

When you read, ask yourself
questions. Try to think of the answers.
It's like talking to yourself about what
you are reading.

Ask questions as you read.

Whose lunch is it?

from *Tuesday's Lunch*
by Edward Marshall

On the other side of the
wall they met a poor old cat.

"I'm so happy," said the old
cat. "A nice lunch fell from
the sky!"

"Three tuna sandwiches?"
said Fox.

"Gosh," said the old cat.
"Kids are really smart these
days."

© GREAT SOURCE. COPYING IS PROHIBITED.

4 Draw What You See

When you read, draw pictures in your head. First, think about what you read. Then, draw a picture of what you see in your head.

Draw a picture of what happened in the story.

> As you read, mark, ask questions, predict, and draw what you see.

© GREAT SOURCE. COPYING IS PROHIBITED.

When you read the stories in this book, remember to be an active reader. Active readers do 4 things.

They will get in trouble.

Whose lunch is it?

1. Mark

"Ugh!" said Carmen. "Tuna fish!"

"Ugh!" said Fox. "Tuna fish!"

"Oh, no!" said Dexter. "Tuna fish!"

2. Predict

"Let's throw our lunches away," said Fox.

"Let's do!" said the others.

3. Ask Questions

"I'm so happy," said the old cat. "A nice lunch fell from the sky!"

4. Draw What You See

© GREAT SOURCE. COPYING IS PROHIBITED.

Reading Stories

A good story has 3 things that keep us reading. A story has **characters** that we get to know. It has **settings** that tell where the story takes place. And a story has a **plot**, which is what happens during the story.

© GREAT SOURCE. COPYING IS PROHIBITED.

Character Clues

Characters are the people or animals in a story. You can learn about characters by what they say or do. Look for clues that tell you what the character is like.

Now read this story about a pig named Amanda.

Underline some things Amanda says or does.

"Growing Up" from
More Tales of Amanda Pig
by Jean Van Leeuwen

"Mother," said Amanda. "What can I do to help you?"

"You can help mix up these muffins for dinner," said mother.

Amanda helped mix up the muffins.

"What a good helper you are getting to be," said Mother.

© GREAT SOURCE. COPYING IS PROHIBITED.

"Growing Up" (continued)

My Notes

"I can do a lot of things," said Amanda. "I am almost grown up, you know. Soon I will be moving out."

"Oh, my," said Mother. "Already? Come and tell me about it while we wait for Father and Oliver."

Mother and Amanda sat in the big chair.

"What do you think you will do when you grow up?" asked Mother.

© GREAT SOURCE. COPYING IS PROHIBITED.

"I will be a ballet dancer," said Amanda. "And a cook and a doctor and I will fly to the moon."

"All at once?" said Mother. "You will be busy."

"I am going to be very busy when I grow up," said Amanda.

"Where will you live," asked Mother, "when you are not on the moon?"

"I will build a house next door to you," said Amanda.

"And I will do whatever I want whenever I want to do it. I will wear perfume all the time and go to bed at midnight and never eat eggs."

© GREAT SOURCE. COPYING IS PROHIBITED.

What does Amanda say?

What do you learn?

What does Amanda do?

What do you learn?

© GREAT SOURCE. COPYING IS PROHIBITED.

What are 3 words that describe Amanda?

_____

- -

_____

- -

_____

_____

- -

_____

What are 3 words that describe you?

_____

- -

_____

- -

_____

_____

- -

_____

© GREAT SOURCE. COPYING IS PROHIBITED.

➥Use your ideas to write about Amanda. Tell some things you learned about her. How are you like her? How are you not like her?

_____

_____

_____

_____

_____

_____

_____

_____

_____

_____

_____

_____

_____

_____

_____

_____

_____

_____

_____

_____

© GREAT SOURCE. COPYING IS PROHIBITED.

Watch what characters in a story say and do.

19

2 Where Are We?

The place where a story happens is called the **setting**. Look for clues about *when* and *where* a story takes place.

Now read this story about a boy named Henry and his dog Mudge.

Circle words that tell when or where.

from *Henry and Mudge Under the Yellow Moon*
by Cynthia Rylant

In the (fall,) Henry and his big dog Mudge took long walks in the woods.

Henry loved looking at the tops of the trees. He liked the leaves: orange, yellow, brown, and red.

Mudge loved sniffing at the ground. And he liked the leaves, too. He always ate a few.

© GREAT SOURCE. COPYING IS PROHIBITED.

from ***Henry and Mudge Under the Yellow Moon*** (continued)

My Notes

In the fall, Henry liked counting the birds flying south. Mudge liked watching for busy chipmunks.

Since one was a boy and the other was a dog, they never did things just the same way.

Henry picked apples and Mudge licked apples.

Henry put on a coat and Mudge grew one. And when the fall wind blew, Henry's ears turned red and Mudge's ears turned inside out.

© GREAT SOURCE. COPYING IS PROHIBITED.

My Notes

from **Henry and Mudge Under the Yellow Moon** (continued)

But one thing about them was the same. In the fall Henry and Mudge liked being together, most of all.

What words tell you <u>when</u> the story takes place?

_____

_____

_____

_____

What words tell you <u>where</u> the story takes place?

_____

_____

_____

_____

© GREAT SOURCE. COPYING IS PROHIBITED.

◗◗ Now draw a picture of the setting.
Then write about when and where it is.

© GREAT SOURCE. COPYING IS PROHIBITED.

As you read, note
when and where the
story takes place.

3 What Is Happening?

Every story has a beginning, a middle, and an end. What happens in these three parts makes up the **plot**.

Now read this story. Look for how it begins. Then think about how it ends.

As you read, ask yourself questions like: What will happen next?

Write questions about what will happen next.

Who will be scared?

"The Scary Movie" from
The Adventures of Sugar and Junior
by Angela Shelf Medearis

Sugar and Junior went to the movies. They paid for their tickets.

"I know all about this movie," Junior said. "My friend Ramón told me about it."

"Is it scary?" asked Sugar.

"It's real scary. But don't worry. I'll hold your hand."

"Does it have monsters in it?" asked Sugar.

"It has lots of monsters in it. But don't be scared, Sugar. I'll hold your hand."

© GREAT SOURCE. COPYING IS PROHIBITED.

"The Scary Movie" (continued)

My Notes

They found seats close to the front.

"This movie is going to make you scream," said Junior.

Soon the movie started. It was scary. It had lots of monsters. Someone kept screaming and screaming.

It was Junior. He screamed every time he saw a monster.

"Junior," said Sugar, "please stop screaming. I can't hear."

Junior hid his face behind his hands. He hid behind the seats. He screamed and he screamed.

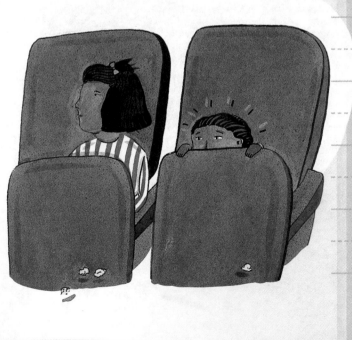

© GREAT SOURCE. COPYING IS PROHIBITED.

"The Scary Movie" (continued)

"Junior," said Sugar, "please stop screaming. The movie is over. Everyone has left but us."

"See?" said Junior as he crawled from under the seat. "I told you it was a scary movie."

"I think I like scary movies," said Sugar.

It was getting dark outside.

"Do you think there are scary monsters in the dark?" asked Junior.

"Yes," Sugar said, "but don't worry. I'll hold your hand, all the way home."

And she did.

© GREAT SOURCE. COPYING IS PROHIBITED.

●◆Fill in this chart about the plot in this story.

●◆What happens in the beginning?

●◆What things happen in the middle of the story?

●◆What happens at the end?

© GREAT SOURCE. COPYING IS PROHIBITED.

On the lines below, tell about something that happened to you and a friend. Tell what happened first, in the middle, and at the end in your story.

First

_____

_____

_____

_____

Middle

_____

_____

_____

_____

At the end

_____

_____

_____

_____

Look for what happens in the beginning, middle, and end of a story.

© GREAT SOURCE. COPYING IS PROHIBITED.

© GREAT SOURCE. COPYING IS PROHIBITED.

Reading Nonfiction

Writing about real people and things is called **nonfiction**. It's true, not made up. You read nonfiction to learn things. You can learn lots of facts and details from nonfiction.

As you read nonfiction, look for the big main ideas as well as the details.

Looking for the Main Idea

The **main idea** is the writer's big idea. Details are bits of information that tell you more about the main idea. When you read nonfiction, look for the main idea and for details.

As you read, mark the most important idea and 2 or 3 details.

from *The Sun Is Always Shining Somewhere*
by Allan Fowler

The sun never stops shining.

Do you know why you can't see the sun at night? To find the answer, turn on a lamp in a dark room.

Put a tiny mark on a ball. Pretend the mark is you. Imagine the ball is the Earth.

© GREAT SOURCE. COPYING IS PROHIBITED.

from **The Sun Is Always Shining Somewhere** (continued)

EARTH

BASKETBALL

Now hold the ball in front of the lamp. Slowly turn the ball around.

The part of it that was lit up by the lamp before is now in the dark. The part that was dark before is now in the light.

Earth is like a ball—a very big ball. It is always turning.

It turns out of the sunlight and into the dark of night, then back into the sunlight the next morning.

Isn't this nice to know?

Even when you're asleep at night, the sun is always shining—somewhere.

SUN

© GREAT SOURCE. COPYING IS PROHIBITED.

●◆What is this reading about? Put an X in front of all right answers.

◯ sun   ◯ sleep

◯ Earth   ◯ bed

●◆Find 1 sentence from this reading that tells what it is all about. Copy that sentence below.

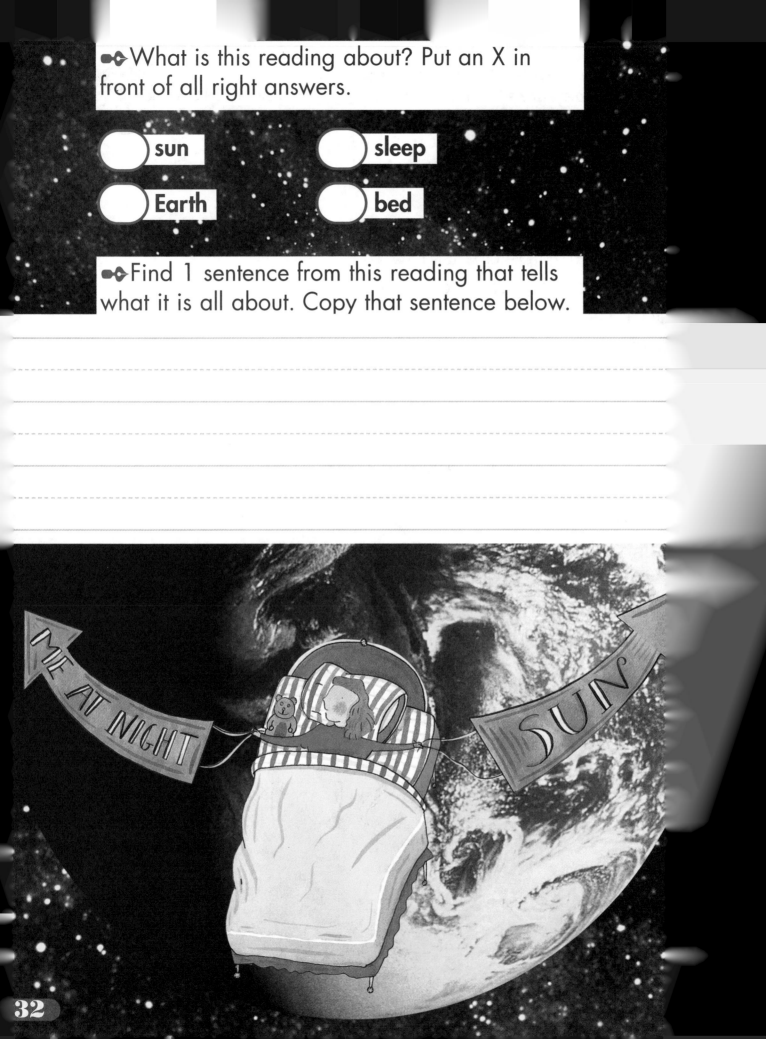

ME AT NIGHT

SUN

☛ Now tell what the reading is about. Start with the big idea you wrote on page 32.

2 Big Ideas and Small

Some ideas are big and important. Other ideas are less important. When you read, look for the big, or main, idea. That's the author's main message. Less important ideas are called details. They tell you things about the main idea.

On each page, mark and write 1 detail. Circle the main idea.

Germs are tiny.

From **Germs Make Me Sick!**
by Melvin Berger

You wake up one morning. But you don't feel like getting out of bed. Your arms and legs ache. Your head hurts. You have a fever. And your throat is sore.

"I'm sick," you say. "I must have caught a germ."

Everyone knows that germs can make you sick. But not everyone knows how.

Germs are tiny living things. They are far too small to see with your eyes alone. In fact, a line of one thousand germs could fit across the top of a pencil!

© GREAT SOURCE. COPYING IS PROHIBITED.

from ***Germs Make Me Sick!***
(continued)

My Notes

There are many different kinds of germs. But the two that usually make you sick are bacteria and viruses.

Under a microscope, some bacteria look like little round balls. Others are as straight as rods. Still others are twisted in spiral shapes.

Viruses are far tinier than bacteria. Some look like balls with spikes sticking out on all sides. Others look like loaves of bread or like tadpoles. There are even some that look like metal screws with spider legs.

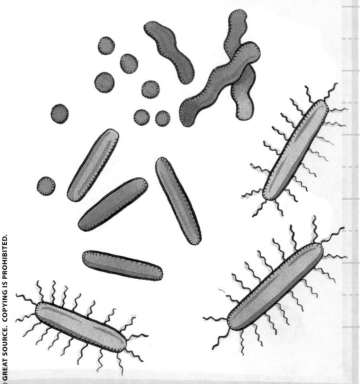

© GREAT SOURCE. COPYING IS PROHIBITED.

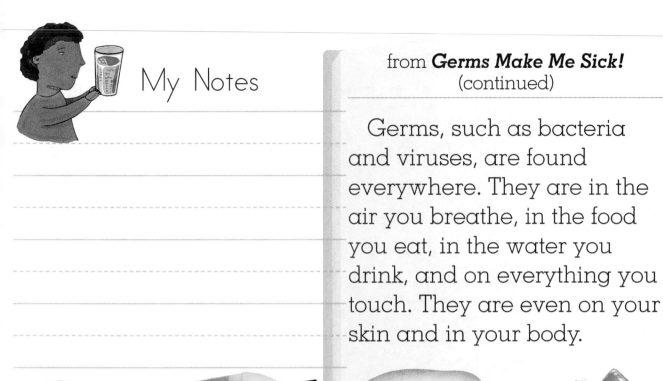

My Notes

Germs, such as bacteria and viruses, are found everywhere. They are in the air you breathe, in the food you eat, in the water you drink, and on everything you touch. They are even on your skin and in your body.

❥ What ONE thing is this reading about?

© GREAT SOURCE. COPYING IS PROHIBITED.

✎➔On the lines, write 3 details from the reading.

1.

2.

3.

✎➔Tell what you learned. Tell the most important thing and 1 or 2 details.

As you read, sort the big ideas from the details.

©GREAT SOURCE. COPYING IS PROHIBITED.

3 What's It About?

When you read, you try to understand what the author is saying. You also try to remember. One way to do that is to retell what you read in your own words.

On each page, write one important point you would tell someone.

from ***Sleep Is for Everyone***
by Paul Showers

When a horse goes to sleep, its eyelids go down. When a chicken goes to sleep, its eyelids go up. When a snake sleeps, its eyes stay open. Snakes have no eyelids.

When you go to sleep, which way do your eyelids go?

© GREAT SOURCE. COPYING IS PROHIBITED.

from **Sleep Is for Everyone**
(continued)

An elephant can sleep standing up. A pigeon sits down when it sleeps. Pigs lie down to sleep. So do dogs. So do you.

Sometimes dogs curl up. So do cats. Cows don't. Do you?

➤Make a web. Write 3 ways animals might sleep.

sleep

© GREAT SOURCE. COPYING IS PROHIBITED.

●►In your own words, tell what you learned about sleep. On the lines, write an important point from each page.

1st page (Look at your notes.)

_____

_____

_____

_____

_____

_____

2nd page (Look at your web.)

_____

_____

_____

_____

_____

As you read, ask yourself, "What is the author saying?"

40

© GREAT SOURCE. COPYING IS PROHIBITED.

Reading Authors

Authors are all different. That's part of what makes books interesting to read.

Here you will read three different authors. Note how each one writes and what words each one uses. Note, too, the different things authors write about.

© GREAT SOURCE. COPYING IS PROHIBITED.

Learning About Characters

Writers make a character seem real. They show how a character looks and acts. They tell what a character likes to do. They describe how a character acts, thinks, and feels.

As you read, write questions about the characters.

What will he do?

from *Jamal's Busy Day*
by Wade Hudson

Mommy, Daddy and I start our work day early. We wash up, shave, and brush our teeth.

Then we put on our work clothes. I always finish first.

Before we leave for work, we eat a healthy breakfast. We have to be ready for our busy day.

© GREAT SOURCE. COPYING IS PROHIBITED.

from **Jamal's Busy Day** (continued)

My Notes

My daddy is an architect. He makes drawings to guide the people who build houses. He works hard.

My mommy is an accountant. She's always busy with numbers. Mommy works very hard.

I work hard, too. I work with numbers. I make drawings. I try experiments. I do research. Then there are meetings to attend.

TODAY'S ASSIGNMENT FOR HOMEWORK IS

© GREAT SOURCE. COPYING IS PROHIBITED.

from **Jamal's Busy Day** (continued)

My supervisor always calls on me for a helping hand. And sometimes I have to settle disagreements between my co-workers. There is always work to do.

Getting home is not easy, either. The bus is always crowded. But when I get there, I relax. I have to unwind.

© GREAT SOURCE. COPYING IS PROHIBITED.

from *Jamal's Busy Day* (continued)

Sometimes I bring work home. Reports are always due.

Then I shoot a few hoops. Soon, it's time for dinner. We all help. I set the table.

Later, Daddy and Mommy talk about their busy day. I say, "I know just what you mean. I've had a busy day myself."

But I can't wait until tomorrow.

© GREAT SOURCE. COPYING IS PROHIBITED.

Use the story boxes below to tell how Jamal acts in the beginning, middle, and end.

First

Next

Last

Note what the characters in a story are like and what they say and do.

© GREAT SOURCE. COPYING IS PROHIBITED.

Authors Choose Words

All writers choose the words they write. The words each writer chooses help make his or her writing different. Words are how writers express themselves.

Circle 1 or 2 words that the author uses to describe things.

from *Truman's Aunt Farm*
by Jama Kim Rattigan

At eleven o'clock a package arrived for Truman. It was a birthday present from Aunt Fran. Truman looked at the box. It was not moving. He gently picked it up. It felt empty. He turned it over, then smelled it. Presents from Aunt Fran had to be handled very carefully.

Truman slowly opened the box. It was empty! No, there were two cards. The yellow one said: "Happy Birthday dear Truman! I am giving you the ant farm you wanted. Love, your charming Aunt Fran."

HAPPY BIRTHDAY dear TRUMAN!

© GREAT SOURCE. COPYING IS PROHIBITED.

MAIL THIS CARD RIGHT AWAY TO RECEIVE YOUR FREE ANTS!

from ***Truman's Aunt Farm***
(continued)

The green one said: "Mail this card right away to receive your free ants! Watch them work! Watch them play! Watch them eat! Live ants!"

Truman mailed his card right away. Oh boy. Live ants! Live ants for his very own!

But he didn't get ants. He got *aunts*.

It was true. There were aunts everywhere. They all loved Truman and made such a fuss!

"My, how you've grown," said Aunt Lulu.

"Isn't he handsome?" said Aunt Jodie.

© GREAT SOURCE. COPYING IS PROHIBITED.

from **Truman's Aunt Farm**
(continued)

"Looks just like me," said Aunt Ramona. And they hugged him, and patted his head, and pinched his cheeks, and talked his ears off.

Dear Charming Aunt Fran,

Thank you for the birthday present.

I have fifty-something aunts at my house now.

More are arriving daily. What shall I do?

Love,
Your bug-loving nephew,
Truman

P.S. What should I feed the aunts?

© GREAT SOURCE. COPYING IS PROHIBITED.

My Notes

from **Truman's Aunt Farm**
(continued)

Truman looked out his front window. A long, long line of aunts was waiting to get in. They brought their knitting and homemade banana bread and gave Truman more than one hundred-something gift subscriptions to children's magazines.

"Help!" yelled Truman.

"Letter for you," said the postman.

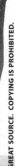

© GREAT SOURCE. COPYING IS PROHIBITED.

from **Truman's Aunt Farm**
(continued)

My dear Truman,

I am glad you liked the present. Don't let those ants bug you. Do you have any friends who would like some ants?

Love,
Your clever Aunt Fran

P.S. Feed the ants ant food.

◆ List 3 words the writer uses that you liked best. Tell why you liked them.

1.

2.

3.

© GREAT SOURCE. COPYING IS PROHIBITED.

➥ Now write a letter of your own to Aunt Fran. Tell her what you think of the story so far.

Dear Aunt _____,

Love,

Notice the words a writer uses in a story.

52

© GREAT SOURCE. COPYING IS PROHIBITED.

3 What a Problem!

Writers tell stories. Stories often show a **problem** and how it is solved. In this story, a mouse has a problem. As you read, watch how the mouse solves her problem.

As you read, draw pictures of the problem and how it's solved.

from "The Wishing Well"
by Arnold Lobel

A mouse once found a wishing well.

"Now all of my wishes can come true!" she cried.

She threw a penny into the well and made a wish.

"OUCH!" said the wishing well.

mouse

© GREAT SOURCE. COPYING IS PROHIBITED.

from **"The Wishing Well"**
(continued)

The next day the mouse came back to the well. She threw a penny into the well and made a wish.

"OUCH!" said the well.

The next day the mouse came back again. She threw a penny into the well.

"I wish this well would not say ouch," she said.

"OUCH!" said the well. "That hurts!"

© GREAT SOURCE. COPYING IS PROHIBITED.

from **"The Wishing Well"**
(continued)

"What shall I do?" cried the mouse. "My wishes will never ever come true this way!"

The mouse ran home. She took the pillow from her bed.

"This may help," said the mouse, and she ran back to the well.

The mouse threw the pillow into the well. Then she threw a penny into the well and made a wish.

© GREAT SOURCE. COPYING IS PROHIBITED.

from **"The Wishing Well"**
(continued)

"Ah. That feels much better!" said the well.

"Good!" said the mouse. "Now I can start wishing."

After that day the mouse made many wishes by the well.

And every one of them came true.

© GREAT SOURCE. COPYING IS PROHIBITED.

What problem did the mouse have?

Problem

Solution

How did the mouse solve her problem?

© GREAT SOURCE. COPYING IS PROHIBITED.

Make a book cover for this story. On the cover, show the problem that the mouse has in this story.

Look for the problem and how it's solved in a story.

© GREAT SOURCE. COPYING IS PROHIBITED.

Reading Poetry

Poems use words and sounds to show feelings. Some poems rhyme, and some don't.

Poets choose their words to make readers feel a certain way. Poets want readers to imagine the ideas in their poems.

Here you'll ask questions about poems and picture ideas in your mind.

© GREAT SOURCE. COPYING IS PROHIBITED.

Time . . . Dime . . . Rhyme!

HOW DOES IT SOUND?

When sounds repeat at the end of a line of poetry, they **rhyme**. Rhyme makes poetry fun to read.

Read this poem. How does it sound? How does the rhyme make you feel?

As you read, circle some words in the poem that <u>rhyme</u>.

"Changing"
by Mary Ann Hoberman

I know what *I* feel like;
I'd like to be (you)
And feel what *you* feel like
And do what *you* (do.)

© GREAT SOURCE. COPYING IS PROHIBITED.

"Changing" (continued)

I'd like to change places
For maybe a week
And look like your look-like
And speak as you speak
And think what you're thinking
And go where you go
And feel what you're feeling
And know what you know.
I wish we could do it;
What fun it would be
If I could try you out
And you could try me.

My Notes

Write some of the rhyming words in the poem.

<u>You</u> rhymes with

<u>Speak</u> rhymes with

<u>Be</u> rhymes with

© GREAT SOURCE. COPYING IS PROHIBITED.

➨Write a word that rhymes with each word below.

free
_____

weak
_____

snow
_____

day
_____

Note that some sounds in a poem rhyme, or sound the same.

© GREAT SOURCE. COPYING IS PROHIBITED.

Poets use words and sounds in a poem to show feeling. The words can sound happy, sad, or scary.

Read this poem about a girl with a giggle.

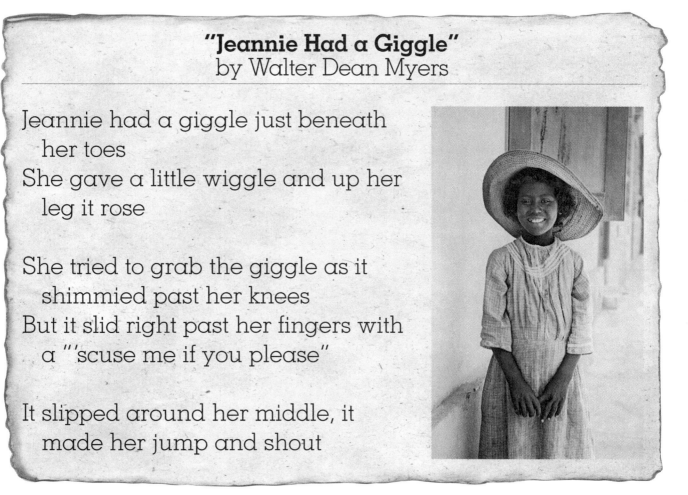

"Jeannie Had a Giggle"
by Walter Dean Myers

Jeannie had a giggle just beneath
  her toes
She gave a little wiggle and up her
  leg it rose

She tried to grab the giggle as it
  shimmied past her knees
But it slid right past her fingers with
  a "'scuse me if you please"

It slipped around her middle, it
made her jump and shout

Write on the lines how the words make you feel.

This makes me feel

© GREAT SOURCE. COPYING IS PROHIBITED.

Jeannie wanted that giggle in, that giggle wanted out!
Jeannie closed her mouth, but then she heard a funny
  sound
As out that silly giggle flew and jumped down to the
  ground

Jeannie caught it with her foot just beneath her toes
She gave a little wiggle and up her leg it rose

How do these words make you feel?

My Notes

➦Write 2 or 3 of your favorite words from the poem.

Now read this poem about the moon.

The moon has a glow
A warm, shiny light
That tickles the shadows
And softens the light

© GREAT SOURCE. COPYING IS PROHIBITED.

➤Let's have fun with words! In the shape below, finish this poem about the sun. Use your favorite words to show feelings. Your poem can rhyme—or not! It's your choice!

The sun

is _____

_____

and looks so_____

_____.

It glows and_____

_____

And makes me feel

_____

_____.

When you read poems, think about how the words make you feel.

© GREAT SOURCE. COPYING IS PROHIBITED.

3 Word Pictures

Poets pick their words so that you can "see" their ideas.

Read this poem about summertime. Picture the words in your head as you read them. What do the words make you see?

Draw some things you see in the poem.

"Big Plans" by Nikki Grimes

School is out soon
and Danitra's advice is:
surrender
to
summer,
to
raspberry ices
and
pink lemonade
and
walks on the beach

© GREAT SOURCE. COPYING IS PROHIBITED.

"Big Plans" (continued)

and
at least
one
trip to the zoo,
one
Ferris wheel ride,
one
family barbecue,
one
Sunday school picnic,
but
never a lick
of
homework to spoil
one
afternoon.

My Notes

© GREAT SOURCE. COPYING IS PROHIBITED.

1. Go back to the poem. Circle any words you can picture in your mind.

2. Write 3 things from the poem that you can see, and then draw pictures of them.

3. What is your favorite season? Circle it.

     Fall   Winter   Spring   Summer

4. Write 2 or 3 words that help you picture your favorite season. Then draw it in the box.

© GREAT SOURCE. COPYING IS PROHIBITED

●→Use the words you wrote to make a poem about your favorite season.

My
favorite season
is _____ .
Because it makes
me _____

When you read poetry, picture the words in your mind.

70

© GREAT SOURCE. COPYING IS PROHIBITED.

Reading Nonfiction

Nonfiction writing is about real things. It tells about real people and real things that have happened.

Here you'll read some nonfiction. You'll learn about real people and real things, like elephants and bubbles.

© GREAT SOURCE. COPYING IS PROHIBITED.

What Does It Mean?

Readers always ask themselves questions. They retell important ideas in their own words.

Nonfiction writing teaches us things. As you read, notice the important ideas and ask yourself, "What is this writer trying to teach me?"

As you read, <u>underline</u> important ideas.

from ***The Elephant***
by Paula Z. Hogan

<u>Elephants eat almost all day long.</u> They are the largest animals on land. Even their babies weigh more than a full-grown man.

A newborn elephant tries to walk right after birth. At first it trips and falls. Two days later a baby can keep up with the adults.

The mother elephant gives milk to her baby. She must watch it carefully. Lions might hunt for small elephants.

© GREAT SOURCE. COPYING IS PROHIBITED.

from **The Elephant** (continued)

Baby elephants are always in trouble. They have play fights and climb over grown-ups. Sometimes they get stuck in the mud.

Several elephants live in a herd. All the adults help care for the baby. An older female leads the herd.

The leader looks out for danger. If lions are near, she moves her herd away. At times she attacks the lions.

Elephants are very friendly. They greet each other by touching with their trunks. Herds sometimes join together.

© GREAT SOURCE. COPYING IS PROHIBITED.

from **The Elephant** (continued)

Young elephants must learn to drink with their trunks. They suck up water and pour it into their mouths.

When they are about two years old, young elephants begin to grow tusks. They can use tusks to push down trees. That's how elephants eat leaves from the highest branches.

On hot days elephants rest in the shade. They keep cool by spraying water on their backs.

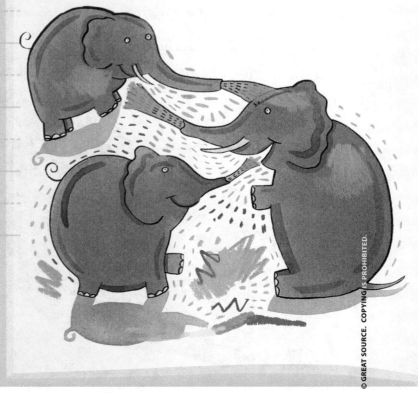

© GREAT SOURCE. COPYING IS PROHIBITED.

✏️ Write 2 or 3 important things you learned about elephants.

_____

_____

_____

_____

_____

_____

✏️ Put an X next to each detail that is true.

☐ Baby elephants are bigger than a person.

☐ Baby elephants drink milk.

☐ Elephants can talk like people do.

☐ Elephants live together in a herd.

☐ Elephants drink with their trunks.

☐ Elephants can push down trees.

☐ Most elephants like cold weather.

©GREAT SOURCE. COPYING IS PROHIBITED.

Use the details you underlined to write a sign for elephants at the zoo. Fill in the first sentence about elephants. Then, write 2 details about elephants.

ELEPHANTS

Elephants are

As you read, ask, "What is this all about?"

© GREAT SOURCE. COPYING IS PROHIBITED.

2 Know What Happens

In nonfiction, writers may tell about what happens in order. They tell what happens first, second, third, and last.

Read about the life cycle of alligators. Note the order in which things happen.

from *The Alligator*
by Sabrina Crewe

The alligator eggs are in the nest. It is summer. The alligator has laid her eggs in a hole on top of her nest. Now she will cover the eggs with leaves and twigs. Inside the eggs, baby alligators are growing.

The alligator keeps guard. The alligator watches carefully over her nest. She will stop any predators from taking her eggs. The eggs are kept warm by the sun and the cover of rotting plants.

Write 2 or 3 things that happen.

She lays eggs.

© GREAT SOURCE. COPYING IS PROHIBITED.

from **The Alligator** (continued)

The baby alligators come out of their eggs. After about two months, the hard shell of the egg starts to crack. Under the hard shell is another, tough layer. Baby alligators use a special tooth on their snouts to cut through the tough layer. Then they hatch from their eggs.

The baby alligators are very small. The baby alligators are only 9 inches (22 cm) long when they hatch. They have black bodies with pale yellow marks. The baby alligators call for help from inside the nest. When she hears their calls, the mother alligator uncovers the nest.

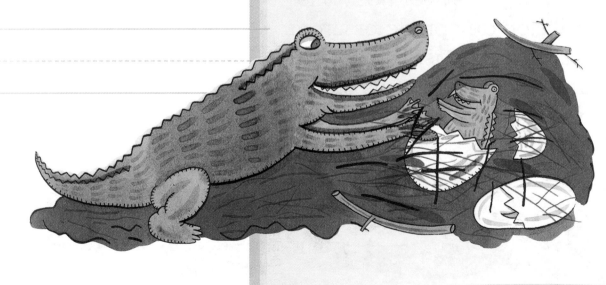

© GREAT SOURCE. COPYING IS PROHIBITED.

from ***The Alligator*** (continued)

The mother alligator carries her babies. The mother alligator scoops the babies into her large mouth. She takes them from the nest to the edge of the pool. Then she drops them in the water. The mother makes several trips to get all the babies to the pool.

The baby alligators can swim well. Baby alligators can swim from the moment they hatch. In the water, they are safe from land animals. But they may be caught by birds, fish, or snakes.

© GREAT SOURCE. COPYING IS PROHIBITED.

What happens first? What happens next? Write the order things happen in an alligator's life.

What happens first?

1.

What happens second?

2.

© GREAT SOURCE. COPYING IS PROHIBITED.

What happens after that?

3.

What happens last?

4. Mother alligator carries the babies to the water.

Look for the order of things as you read.

© GREAT SOURCE. COPYING IS PROHIBITED.

3 Read to Understand

Nonfiction writing always tells about something. The subject of a piece of writing is called a **topic**. As you read, look for details about the topic.

Now read this passage about bubbles.

As you read, underline important details on each page.

from ***Pop! A Book About Bubbles***
by Kimberly Brubaker Bradley

Dip the plastic wand into the soap solution.

Hold it up to your mouth. Now blow.

Phhhh! You've made a bubble!

Watch it float higher and higher.

The bubble shimmers in the sun.

Up it goes, up, up, then *pop!*

It disappears.

You can blow small bubbles or big ones.

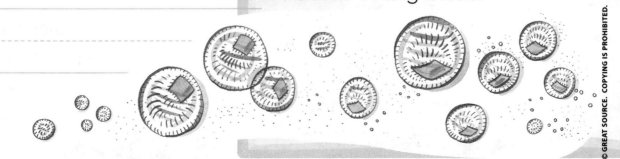

© GREAT SOURCE. COPYING IS PROHIBITED.

from **Pop! A Book About Bubbles**
(continued)

My Notes

You can blow one bubble or hundreds of bubbles.

You can't blow square bubbles or flat bubbles.

All bubbles are round.

Bubbles are air trapped inside liquid.

The liquid you put your bubble wand into is made of water and soap. Sometimes it has a little corn syrup too.

It is sticky. It sticks to the floor if you spill it. It sticks to your fingers when you touch it. And it sticks to the plastic bubble wand. It sticks and it stretches. It stretches across the round hole on the end of the bubble wand.

© GREAT SOURCE. COPYING IS PROHIBITED.

from *Pop! A Book About Bubbles*
(continued)

When you blow into the wand, you make air move.

If you blow slowly, you can see how the air makes the soap on the wand start to s-t-r-e-t-c-h.

As you blow harder, the soap stretches and stretches until it can't stretch anymore.

Finally it snaps free. The soap shuts around the air inside it. There it is!

A bubble!

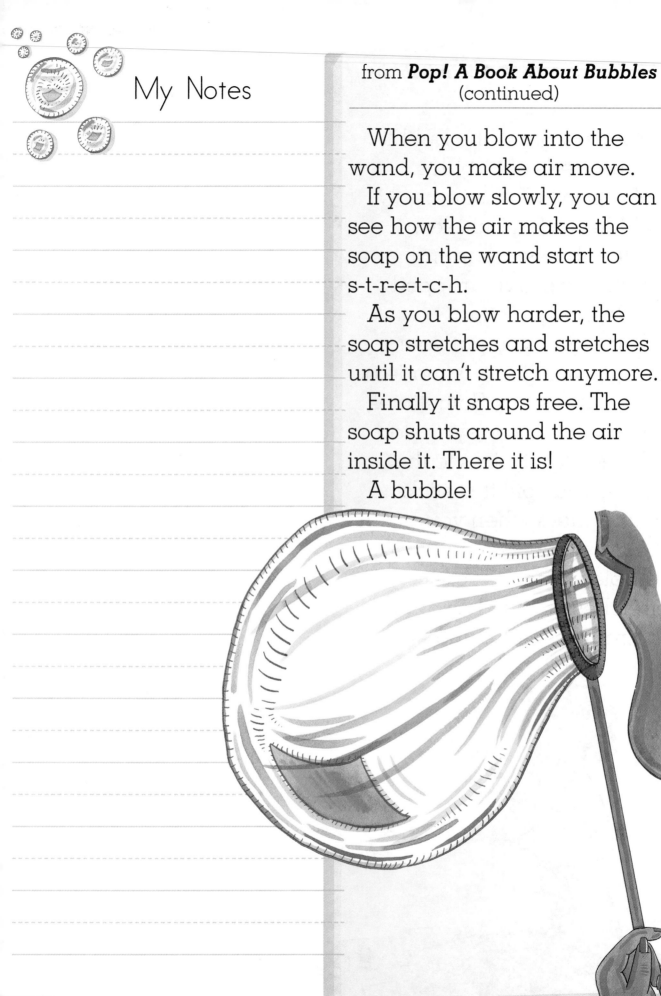

© GREAT SOURCE. COPYING IS PROHIBITED.

➡️Complete the web below. What 3 steps do you take to make bubbles?

1.

Bubbles

2.

3.

© GREAT SOURCE. COPYING IS PROHIBITED.

●→Explain to a friend how to blow bubbles.
Use the notes you wrote on page 85.
Pretend your friend has NEVER done this.

Make a web to
help you understand
what you read.

© GREAT SOURCE. COPYING IS PROHIBITED.

Reading Authors

Authors tell stories. They make up characters. In many stories, the characters have a problem. The story usually ends when they solve the problem.

As you read, watch for the problem in a story. Try to guess what will happen next. Ask, "Is this like something I know about?"

©GREAT SOURCE. COPYING IS PROHIBITED.

Usually the characters in a story have a problem. As a reader, you watch to see what will happen and how the problem is solved.

Now read *Too Many Tamales*. In this story, a girl has a big problem. Have you ever had a problem like this one?

At the end of each page, ask a question about what will happen.

What are they making?

from ***Too Many Tamales***
by Gary Soto

Snow drifted through the streets and now that it was dusk, Christmas trees glittered in the windows.

Maria moved her nose off the glass and came back to the counter. She was acting grown-up now, helping her mother make tamales. Their hands were sticky with <u>masa</u>.

"That's very good," her mother said.

Maria happily kneaded the masa.

masa—food made from corn.

© GREAT SOURCE. COPYING IS PROHIBITED.

from **Too Many Tamales** (continued)

My Notes

She felt grown-up, wearing her mother's apron. Her mom had even let her wear lipstick and perfume. If only I could wear Mom's ring, she thought to herself.

Maria's mother had placed her diamond ring on the kitchen counter. Maria loved that ring. She loved how it sparkled, like their Christmas tree lights.

When her mother left the kitchen to answer the telephone, Maria couldn't help herself. She wiped her hands on the apron and looked back at the door.

"I'll wear the ring for just a minute," she said to herself.

The ring sparkled on her thumb.

© GREAT SOURCE. COPYING IS PROHIBITED.

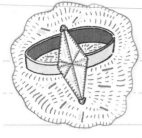

My Notes

Maria returned to kneading the *masa*, her hands pumping up and down. On her thumb the ring disappeared, then reappeared in the sticky glob of dough.

Her mother returned and took the bowl from her. "Go get your father for this part," she said.

Then the three of them began to spread *masa* onto corn husks. Maria's father helped by plopping a spoonful of meat in the center and folding the husk. He then placed them in a large pot on the stove.

© GREAT SOURCE. COPYING IS PROHIBITED.

from *Too Many Tamales* (continued)

They made twenty-four tamales as the windows grew white with delicious-smelling curls of steam.

A few hours later the family came over with armfuls of bright presents: her grandparents, her uncle and aunt, and her cousins Dolores, Teresa, and Danny.

Maria kissed everyone hello. Then she grabbed Dolores by the arm and took her upstairs to play, with the other cousins tagging along after them.

© GREAT SOURCE. COPYING IS PROHIBITED.

from **Too Many Tamales** (continued)

They cut pictures from the newspaper, pictures of toys they were hoping were wrapped and sitting underneath the Christmas tree. As Maria was snipping out a picture of a pearl necklace, a shock spread through her body.

"The ring!" she screamed.

Everyone stared at her. "What ring?" Dolores asked.

Without answering, Maria ran to the kitchen.

© GREAT SOURCE. COPYING IS PROHIBITED.

from **Too Many Tamales** (continued)

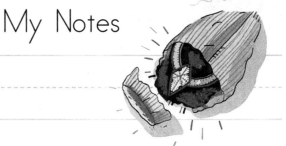

The steaming tamales lay piled on a platter. The ring is inside one of the tamales, she thought to herself. It must have come off when I was kneading the *masa*.

Dolores, Teresa, and Danny skidded into the kitchen behind her.

"Help me!" Maria cried.

They looked at each other. Danny piped up first. "What do you want us to do?"

"Eat them," she said. "If you bite something hard, tell me."

© GREAT SOURCE. COPYING IS PROHIBITED.

➥ Fill out the chart below. First, write the problem in the top box.

Problem

Solution

➥ Now write how you think the problem will be solved.

SOURCE. COPYING IS PROHIBITED.

Have *you* ever lost something? What happened? Did you find it? Write about your problem and how you solved it below.

Look for the problem and how it is solved in a story.

© GREAT SOURCE. COPYING IS PROHIBITED.

As you read, ask yourself, "What do I think of this story?" One way to do that is to **connect** it to your life. Ask yourself, "How is this story like something I know?"

As you read, write how the story is like something in your life.

I have a pond.

from *Dear Mr. Blueberry*
by Simon James

Dear Mr. Blueberry,
I love whales very much and I think I saw one in my pond today. Please send me some information on whales, as I think he might be hurt.
Love,
Emily

Dear Emily,
Here are some details about whales. I don't think you'll find it was a whale you saw, because whales don't live in ponds, but in salt water.

Yours sincerely
Your teacher,
Mr. Blueberry

© GREAT SOURCE. COPYING IS PROHIBITED.

from **Dear Mr. Blueberry** (continued)

My Notes

Dear Mr. Blueberry,

I am now putting salt into the pond every day before breakfast and last night I saw my whale smile. I think he is feeling better.

Do you think he might be lost?

Love,
Emily

Dear Emily,

Please don't put any more salt in the pond. I'm sure your parents won't be pleased.

I'm afraid there can't be a whale in your pond, because whales don't get lost, they always know where they are in the oceans.

Yours sincerely,
Mr. Blueberry

© GREAT SOURCE. COPYING IS PROHIBITED.

How is this story like something in your life?

_____

_____

_____

_____

_____

_____

What did you think of the story? Write
your opinion of the story here.

_____

_____

_____

_____

_____

_____

_____

© GREAT SOURCE. COPYING IS PROHIBITED.

What did you think about this story? Check your opinion of the story. Then write 2 reasons why you liked or didn't like the story.

Title

My Book Review

☐ I liked *Dear Mr. Blueberry* for 2 reasons.

☐ I didn't like *Dear Mr. Blueberry* for 2 reasons.

1.

2.

As you read, ask yourself, "What do I think about this story?"

© GREAT SOURCE. COPYING IS PROHIBITED.

Authors put **messages** in their stories. They write stories to tell you what they think.

As you read *Owl Moon*, ask yourself what the author might be trying to tell you.

In the notes part, write what the author is telling you.

It will be about an owl.

from **Owl Moon** by Jane Yolen

The owl's call came closer, from high up in the trees on the edge of the meadow.

Nothing in the meadow moved.

All of a sudden an owl shadow, part of the big tree shadow, lifted off and flew right over us.

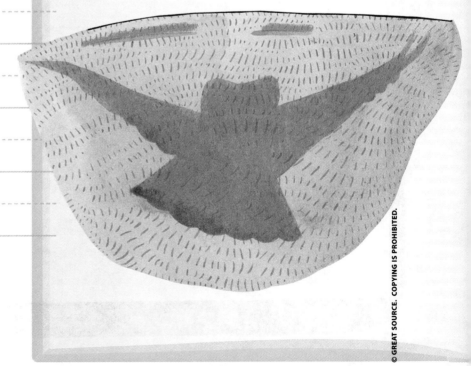

© GREAT SOURCE. COPYING IS PROHIBITED.

from **Owl Moon** (continued)

My Notes

We watched silently with heat in our mouths, the heat of all those words we had not spoken.

The shadow hooted again.

Pa turned on his big flashlight and caught the owl just as it was landing on a branch.

For one minute, three minutes, maybe even a hundred minutes, we stared at one another.

© GREAT SOURCE. COPYING IS PROHIBITED.

My Notes

from **Owl Moon** (continued)

Then the owl pumped its great wings and lifted off the branch like a shadow without sound.

It flew back into the forest.

"Time to go home," Pa said to me.

I knew then I could talk, I could even laugh out loud. But I was a shadow as we walked home.

102

© GREAT SOURCE. COPYING IS PROHIBITED.

from **Owl Moon** (continued)

My Notes

When you go owling you don't need words or warm or anything but hope. That's what Pa says.

The kind of hope that flies on silent wings under a shining Owl Moon.

© GREAT SOURCE. COPYING IS PROHIBITED.

✒️ What is the writer trying to say? Write what these sentences from *Owl Moon* mean to you.

"Then the owl pumped its great wings and lifted off the branch like a shadow without sound."

_____

_____

_____

_____

_____

_____

"When you go owling you don't need words or warm or anything but hope."

_____

_____

_____

_____

_____

_____

© GREAT SOURCE. COPYING IS PROHIBITED.

In the space below, write your own story about an animal. What happens? How does it end?

Title:

As you read, ask, "What is the author trying to say to me?"

© GREAT SOURCE. COPYING IS PROHIBITED.

characters, the people or animals in a story.

connect, to ask how a story is like your life or something you know.

main idea, the writer's big idea.

The sun never stops shining.

messages, what authors put in their stories to tell you what they think.

The kind of hope that flies on silent wings under a shining Owl Moon.

nonfiction, writing about real people and things.

plot, what happens in the beginning, middle, and end of a story.

beginning   middle   end

problem, something that a character has to solve.

rhyme, sounds repeating, like *do* and *you.*

setting, the place where a story happens.

topic, subject of a piece of writing.

© GREAT SOURCE. COPYING IS PROHIBITED.

8 "Tuesday's Lunch" from *Fox All Week* by Edward Marshall, pictures by James Marshall, copyright © 1984 by Edward Marshall, text. Used by permission of Dial Books for Young Readers, an imprint of Penguin Putnam Books for Young Readers, a division of Penguin Putnam Inc. All rights reserved.

14 "Growing Up" from *More Tales of Amanda Pig* by Jean Van Leeuwen, pictures by Ann Schweninger, copyright © 1985 by Jean Van Leeuwen, text. Used by permission of Dial Books for Young Readers, an imprint of Penguin Putnam Books for Young Readers, a division of Penguin Putnam Inc. All rights reserved.

20 From *Henry and Mudge Under the Yellow Moon* by Cynthia Rylant. Reprinted with the permission of Simon & Schuster Books for Young Readers, an imprint of Simon & Schuster Children's Publishing Division from *Henry and Mudge Under the Yellow Moon* by Cynthia Rylant. Text copyright © 1987 Cynthia Rylant.

24 "The Scary Movie" from *The Adventures of Sugar and Junior* by Angela Shelf Medearis. Text copyright © 1995 by Angela Shelf Medearis. All rights reserved. Reprinted from *The Adventures of Sugar and Junior* by permission of Holiday House, Inc.

30 From *The Sun Is Always Shining Somewhere* by Allan Fowler. Copyright © 1991 by Children's Press,® Inc.

34 From *Germs Make Me Sick!* By Melvin Berger. Text Copyright © 1985, 1995 by Melvin Berger. Used by permission of HarperCollins Publishers.

38 From *Sleep Is For Everyone* by Paul Showers. Text Copyright © 1974 by Paul Showers. Used by permission of HarperCollins Publishers.

42 *Jamal's Busy Day,* written by Wade Hudson, illustrated by George Ford and © 1994 by Just Us Books, Inc. Reprinted by permission of the publisher.

47 From *Truman's Aunt Farm* by Jama Kim Rattigan. Text copyright © 1994 by Jama Rattigan. Reprinted by permission of Houghton Mifflin Company. All rights reserved.

53 "The Wishing Well" from *Mouse Tales* by Arnold Lobel. Copyright © 1972 by Arnold Lobel. Used by permission of HarperCollins Publishers.

60 "Changing" from *The Llama Who Had No Pajama: 100 Favorite Poems*, copyright © 1981 Mary Ann Hoberman, reprinted by permission of Harcourt, Inc.

63 "Jeannie Had a Giggle" from *Brown Angels: An Album of Pictures and Verse* by Walter Dean Myers. Copyright © 1993 by Walter Dean Myers. Used by permission of HarperCollins Publishers.

66 "Big Plans" from *Danitra Brown Leaves Town* by Nikki Grimes. Copyright © 2002 by Nikki Grimes. Used by permission of HarperCollins Publishers.

© GREAT SOURCE. COPYING IS PROHIBITED.

72 From *The Elephant* by Paula Z. Hogan. © Steck-Vaughn Company. All rights reserved. Reprinted with permission from Steck-Vaughn Company, Austin, Texas.

77 From *The Alligator* by Sabrina Crewe. © Steck-Vaughn Company. All rights reserved. Reprinted with permission from Steck-Vaughn Company, Austin, Texas.

82 From *Pop! A Book About Bubbles* by Kimberly Brubaker Bradley. Copyright © 2001 by Kimberly Brubaker Bradley. Used by permission of HarperCollins Publishers.

88 From *Too Many Tamales* by Gary Soto, illustrated by Ed Martinez, copyright © 1993 by Gary Soto, text. Used by permission of G.P. Putnam's Sons, an imprint of Penguin Putnam Books for Young Readers, a division of Penguin Putnam Inc. All rights reserved.

96 From *Dear Mr. Blueberry* by Simon James. Reprinted with the permission of Margaret K. McElderry Books, an imprint of Simon & Schuster Children's Publishing Division, from *Dear Mr. Blueberry* by Simon James. Copyright © 1991 Simon James.

96 From *Dear Mr. Blueberry* by Simon James. Extracts taken from *Dear Greenpeace* © 1991 Simon James. Reproduced by permission of publisher, Walker Books Ltd., London. Published in the US under the title of *Dear Mr. Blueberry* by Simon & Schuster.

100 From *Owl Moon* by Jane Yolen, copyright © 1987 by Jane Yolen, text. Used by permission of Philomel Books, an imprint of Penguin Putnam Books for Young Readers, a division of Penguin Putnam Inc. All rights reserved.

The editors have made every effort to trace the ownership of all copyrighted selections found in this book and to make full acknowledgment for their use. Omissions brought to our attention will be corrected in a subsequent edition.

Book Design: Christine Ronan and Sean O'Neill, Ronan Design

Photographs: Cover © Frans Lanting/Minden Pictures and © Mitsuaki Iwago/Minden Pictures

Illustrations on pages 7, 13, 29, 41, 59, 71, 87 © Lisa Adams. Illustrations on pages 53–56 © Arnold Lobel. All other illustrations © Leslie Cober Gentry.

Developed by Nieman Inc.

© GREAT SOURCE. COPYING IS PROHIBITED.

from *The Alligator*, 77

Berger, Melvin, 34

"Big Plans," 66

Bradley, Kimberly Brubaker, 82

"Changing," 60

Crewe, Sabrina, 77

from *Dear Mr. Blueberry*, 96

from *The Elephant*, 72

Fowler, Allan, 30

from *Germs Make Me Sick!*, 34

Grimes, Nikki, 66

"Growing Up" from *More Tales of Amanda Pig*, 14

from *Henry and Mudge Under the Yellow Moon*, 20

Hoberman, Mary Ann, 60

Hogan, Paula Z., 72

Hudson, Wade, 42

from *Jamal's Busy Day*, 42

James, Simon, 96

"Jeannie Had a Giggle," 63

© GREAT SOURCE. COPYING IS PROHIBITED.

Lobel, Arnold, 53

Marshall, Edward, 8

Medearis, Angela Shelf, 24

Myers, Walter Dean, 63

from *Owl Moon*, 100

from *Pop! A Book About Bubbles*, 82

Rattigan, Jama Kim, 47

Rylant, Cynthia, 20

"The Scary Movie" from *The Adventures of Sugar and Junior*, 24

Showers, Paul, 38

from *Sleep Is for Everyone*, 38

Soto, Gary, 88

from *The Sun Is Always Shining Somewhere*, 30

from *Too Many Tamales*, 88

from *Truman's Aunt Farm*, 47

from *Tuesday's Lunch*, 8

Van Leeuwen, Jean, 14

from "The Wishing Well," 53

Yolen, Jane, 100

© GREAT SOURCE. COPYING IS PROHIBITED.